T0076349

SEND IN
SCHOOLS

SEND IN SCHOOLS

{ Amjad Ali }

1 Oliver's Yard
55 City Road
London EC1Y 1SP

CORWIN
A Sage company
2455 Teller Road
Thousand Oaks, California 91320
(800)233-9936
www.corwin.com

Unit No 323-333, Third Floor, F-Block
International Trade Tower, Nehru Place
New Delhi 110 019

8 Marina View Suite 43-053
Asia Square Tower 1
Singapore 018960

Editor: Delayna Spencer
Editorial assistant: Harry Dixon
Production editor: Victoria Nicholas
Marketing manager: Dilhara Attygalle
Cover design: Wendy Scott
Typeset by: C&M Digitals (P) Ltd, Chennai, India

**Library of Congress Control Number:
2024934145**

British Library Cataloguing in Publication data

A catalogue record for this book is available
from the British Library

ISBN 978-1-5296-2470-0 (pbk)

TABLE OF CONTENTS

ABOUT THIS BOOK   VII
ABOUT THE SERIES   IX
ABOUT THE AUTHOR   XI
ACKNOWLEDGEMENTS   XIII

INTRODUCTION   1

1. WHAT IS SEND?   3
2. LOW-EFFORT, HIGH-IMPACT IDEAS   11
3. UNDER- AND OVER-REPRESENTATION   31
4. NEURODIVERSITY/NEURODIVERGENCE   45
5. WORKING TOGETHER   57
6. SOME HELPFUL RESOURCES   67

BIBLIOGRAPHY   79
INDEX   83

ABOUT THIS BOOK

Special Educational Needs are wide ranging and important to consider. No matter the setting, age, or subject it is imperative for all teachers to be up to date and confident with providing an accessible education for all their students. This little book provides you with the perfect starting point. Packed with essential information and practical ways to support the multitude of needs in your classroom, this book is a must-have for teachers.

This book is:

- authored by an expert SENDCO and consultant
- easy to dip in-and-out of
- full of interactive activities, encouraging you to write into the book and make it your own
- short and can be read in an afternoon.

Find out more at
www.sagepub.co.uk/littleguides

{ ABOUT THE SERIES }

A LITTLE GUIDE FOR TEACHERS series is little in size but big on all the support and inspiration you need to navigate your day-to-day life as a teacher.

IDEAS FOR THE CLASSROOM

HINTS & TIPS

REFLECTION

NOTE THIS DOWN

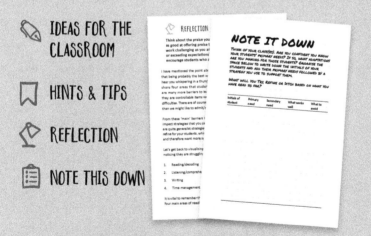

www.sagepub.co.uk/littleguides

ABOUT THE AUTHOR

Amjad Ali (Twitter/X @TeachLeadAAli and Instagram @TryThisTeaching) is a teacher, trainer, TEDx speaker and Senior Leader. He currently works four days a week in a start-up secondary school and offers CPD/INSET on his other day. Amjad has spent his teaching career working in challenging, diverse schools. He is a qualified SENDCO and was also trained as an Advanced Skills Teacher in Teaching and Learning. Before stepping into the world of education, he spent time as a Play Worker and Teaching Assistant in Young Offender prisons.

Amjad has delivered CPD to all sectors in education from Early Careers teachers to Executive/Head Teachers and CEOs, delivering on a range of topics, across the United Kingdom and different parts of the world. He has worked with over 250 schools and thousands of students.

Amjad is the co-founder of the charity The BAMEed Network (#BAMEed) – a grass-roots movement aimed at ensuring diverse communities are represented as a substantive part of the education workforce for teachers and leaders in education. See www.bameednetwork.com for more information.

ACKNOWLEDGEMENTS

Writing a book is not easy and knowing that every word will be scrutinised is a key driving force for labelling oneself an imposter. It has therefore taken me a long time to write down the information in this book in a way that I feel happy with you all reading to yourself, to your peers and to others. The other reason why a book often takes time is due to the messy nature of life, having a young family maybe, and also, for me personally, working four days a week as a senior leader whilst spending the fifth day of every week delivering CPD/keynotes (www.TryThisTeaching.com/CPD) and workshops around the United Kingdom. Wait, what a humble brag, right? Well, not entirely. The reason I am sharing this is because what I have written is what I often share with hundreds of schools and has potentially impacted thousands of students. The ideas that are to be shared have been tried and tested; they are low effort and high impact. These ideas, thoughts and feelings have been wrapped together from my years of teaching and leadership experience, my communications with parents and carers, my years of scanning research and engulfing myself in evidence, through being coached and mentored, and finally, through trial and error. So, use these ideas with a contextual lens and allow me to welcome you to jump into this book with an open mind. If you have found yourself saying, 'well we have always done it this way', my response is a simple one: 'How effective is that way?'. If you can answer positively and with evidence to support your feelings, then, please, carry on, and help others to learn from you.

I cannot go on without a special thank you to all the colleagues that I have learnt from, my work colleagues, those whose ear I can bend, learn from and develop alongside. Another big thank you to the members of my social media network — you have been there for me, through every life event, world event and professional milestone. Also, a big thank you to my parents for always pushing me. Despite my dad being illiterate in English and his home language, he raised a son who is now writing this book. Thank you to my mum who instilled the work ethic in me and my siblings to keep striving, thriving and believing. Finally, and by no means least, my beautiful, intelligent (also a teacher) wife, Kelly, for always being my biggest supporter, for hearing me constantly say, 'I need to finish my book!'. And her always replying, 'You can do it'.

INTRODUCTION

Right, here we go. I will write formally in the introduction so you know that I can actually do it(!) and then I will jump into a conversational tone, because, essentially I want you to think of reading this book as like having a conversation with me, or being in a face-to-face CPD session with me. (You can be, book me in!)

Special Educational Needs and Disabilities (SEND) have been an integral part of the education system since its inception in some shape or guise. However, the recognition that we should be prepared and capable of delivering education in diverse formats is a recent development in the long history of teaching. Outdated and offensive terms such as 'uneducable' have rightfully been consigned to the annals of educational history, replaced by more inclusive language such as 'Special', 'Additional' and 'Different Educational Needs'. These linguistic shifts reflect a broader societal understanding of disability, neurodiversity and mental health, and their importance.

In the past, it was common to hear statements like, 'I can't teach this child' or 'They cannot engage with this subject'. Fortunately, most of us

are evolving from such limiting perspectives. As 'professional learners' – which is how I prefer to refer to educators – we have come to the realisation that diversity enriches our lives, and it is indeed the driving force behind progress.

Today, our approach is shifting. Rather than dismissing students or their potential, we are committing to learning, growing and adapting alongside them. We are recognising that every individual is unique, and our role is to meet them where they are and empower them to achieve their full potential and more. This shift in perspective marks a significant step forward in the world of education, embracing the belief that every learner has something valuable to contribute to our collective journey of knowledge and understanding.

Use this book to kickstart your journey, or to revitalise where you are and to pay it forward to others who need a kick into action too!

Whether you are a teacher, teaching assistant or involved in working in Primary, Secondary, Alternative Provision, Further Education, Higher Education or Special Schools, this is one heartfelt thank you for taking time in investing in yourselves to help our most wonderful students.

CHAPTER 1
WHAT IS SEND?

This chapter explores the ideas:

- Understanding key SEND areas of needs is essential
- Learning about SEND requires time, energy and purpose
- All educators are responsible for teaching SEND students

WHAT IS SEND?

Hello, shwmae, halo, dia dhuit, Salaam. First and foremost, thank you again for choosing to pick up this book to learn more about our wonderful variety of students we have the pleasure to teach daily. As educators, it is of course one of our core jobs to be aware of the needs of all our students; not only should we know what 'labels' are attached to them, we must be able to translate them into what barriers, difficulties and strengths these 'labels' bring with them. So, settle in, grab your highlighter(s), different coloured pens, Post-it notes and let's begin. (You don't really need all of those items!)

Remember, in order for you to get something tangible from this book you need to work out your 'implementation intentions' by deciding what you will Try, Refine or Ditch. **Try**, that is, do now, next lesson, this week, as a result of your reading and understanding. Or what you might want to **Refine**, based on ideas you have been reminded of, or used to use, but just need to refresh, or tweak a little. And finally, what will you now **Ditch**, for example, items you will stop doing, or no longer use. Do remember the ideas, practices and items you chose to ditch should not come from my ideas (!) but from what you are currently doing!

Here's also the thing about doing this – your 'tries' and 'ditches' need to be balanced, otherwise you may not change your habits and will in fact just imbalance the way you are currently teaching further. Therefore keep my motto in mind and only work on 'one tweak a week'. Grab yourself a copy of my editable Try, Refine, Ditch document if you would like to keep notes electronically whilst reading: bit.ly/tryrefineditchdoc

Now ask yourself how you personally get the best from CPD. From reading books? Listening to podcasts? Reading blogs? Observing lessons? Learning from colleagues? What do you usually do to help yourself change your habits? Because in order to move from where you are right now to where you want/need to be, you will need to do something tangible and positive with your thoughts and considerations, which will in turn create an emotional reward/gain for you to be able to maintain it. Changing habits is hard, but you need to see there is a benefit in changing something you are already so intertwined and entrenched in. When you see it makes your life easier, or better or even simpler, then you are more likely to continue. So, after reading each chapter/section you will need to try to set yourself actions and goals with the use of the Try, Refine, Ditch document to help you maintain a change in your undesirable habit to your desirable new habit.

 REFLECTION

Reflect on your previous learning. Jot down the details in the table below. How effective were they?

Name of book	What you learned and did	Name of podcast/blog	What you learned and did

REASONABLE ADJUSTMENTS

Ok, here we go. SEND or Special Educational Needs and Disability, covers a wide range of additional needs that require us to act within the parameters of legislation encapsulated in the SEND Code of Practice (SEND CoP) (see GOV.UK, 2014, and check out the amendments made throughout the years). Under the Equality Act 2010 (GOV.UK, n.d.), we have to make 'reasonable adjustments' (this little phrase is mentioned 17 times in the SEND CoP!). Reasonable, did you say? Adjustments, you shout. Well, yes, reasonably reasonable adjustable adjustments. The interpretation of what constitutes a reasonable adjustment is as complex and confused as that previous sentence structure. Who exactly should be getting these reasonable adjustments or reasonable alterations or adaptations in our lessons? Well, essentially, any student that needs them should get support, but more specifically under the SEND CoP a student with a K code or an E code. Ok, so in order to make these adjustments, we have to differentiate. Scaffold? Or the new buzz word, be 'adaptative' with our teaching, right? But what does that even mean … Do not worry, I've got you! Keep reading…

WHAT DO THOSE LETTERS MEAN?

Well, a student who is on the SEND register with a need under one or more of the four categories of need communication and interaction, cognition and learning, physical disabilities, and social emotional and mental health – will have a K code. Those who have an Education Health Care Plan will have an E Code. Well, that clears it all up then… no? Ok, keep reading then.

Here are the four categories of need as per the SEND CoP:

1.   Communication and Interaction (C&I)

2.   Cognition and Learning (C&L)

3.   Social, Emotional and Mental Health difficulties (SEMHD)

4.   Physical and/or Sensory Needs (P&SN)

Let me go through each of these four categories, **briefly** explaining each one. As this is a **little** guide of SEND, I will never be able to cover information regarding **all** SEND needs, so I will have to tackle items with a broad brush, and approach strategies with generalist strokes. I am not suggesting that other areas are not important, but we have to start somewhere, and I am going to start where there is seemingly a majority of need. However, as I am super generous, I will signpost some links throughout the book to help you discover more information about other areas of need too.

> *Many children and young people have difficulties that fit clearly into one of these areas; some have needs that span two or more areas; for others the precise nature of their need may not be clear at the outset.*
> SEND Code of Practice, GOV.UK (2014)

Let's start with C&I. A student's primary needs could fall into the Communication and Interaction category; however, it is a broad catchment of need that includes conditions that result in challenges with communication and other areas, which can range vastly from social interaction, attention, listening and speaking difficulties. Autism will fall into this category of need. Speech, Communication and Language Needs (SCLN) is arguably one of the biggest areas of needs schools are working with right now.

If a student's main area of difficulty falls under the banner of Cognition and Learning (C&L), it is often a catch-all for students with profound and multiple learning difficulties (PMLD), or moderate learning difficulties (MLD) along with Specific/Severe learning difficulties (SpLD). Conditions like Dyslexia, Dysgraphia, Dyscalculia and Dyspraxia are all examples of SpLDs.

Things becoming clearer yet?

Another category of need is Social, Emotional and Mental Health difficulties which may present themselves through challenging behaviours which are underpinned by mental health issues such as obsessive-compulsive disorder, anxiety, or attachment disorder. These needs could be both mental and sensory. A 'common' condition, ADHD, falls under this category of need.

And finally, Physical and/or Sensory Needs (P&SN). These include hearing impairment, visual impairment, or multi-sensory difficulties. Glasses? Hearing aids? Does that mean all these students should go on the SEND register? Well, no, you would have to decide whether they need something different or additional from what the school is currently offering to support students. Some medical conditions such as diabetes could also fall into this area of need.

These categories of needs were not designed to simply label students into boxes or enable us to provide specific pedagogical approaches within those areas, for example, 'I have an autistic student, does anybody know any SEND specific resources I can use with them?'. SEND needs are not restricted to certain/specific teaching methods or designs. We must take our SEND students as individuals, working with their barriers and strengths to work out which strategies will support development and progress. SEND is not a monolith of similar difficulties, but unique, differing perspectives on what some argue are the norm.

SEND 'LABELS'

Remember I mentioned K and E codes earlier. Well, if students are on the SEND register as needing some form of support in and out of class, they may be on the register under a K code. If their needs are greater and they have had an Educational Health Care Plan (EHCP) applied for (by education, health or families) and provided for them by their Local Authority, they will then have an E code on the SEND register.

But why do you need to know all this? Because, in order for you to be able to support your students effectively you need to know **who** you're supporting and what to do to support them. Additionally, an EHCP is a statutory document, and we are bound by law to ensure the contents are adhered to. Section F in particular is where the support needed to help the person learn is documented.

Just before you think, 'I've got this and I already knew all of the above, so this book was a waste of money' (!) do note that many of the categories above overlap; it would be absolutely normal for us to see difficulties in multiple areas of need! Therefore, remember, you can't simply use it as a checklist of what you know...

Special Educational Needs is a way of addressing a difference, a difficulty, a specialness, a unique, subtle, overt, common, hidden, open, varying way of reading, writing and being in the world that we all seek to flourish in. Society has conditioned us into thinking people with additional needs and/or disabilities are different in a bad way, and that our job is to make them fit in with us, you know neurotypical, able bodied folk. A more positive approach, that I prefer, is to ask whether the world is broadening enough to be accessible and accepting of everyone's differences, as surely it is easier for us to adapt and tweak our lives to invite others in? This is what I seek to show in this book.

Please do not say 'you are a little autistic' because of some ridiculous association with liking routines, for example. And/or please don't say that you are 'a little dyslexic' if you once read a date the wrong way around. Or finally, my favourite, which makes it my worst, 'I am so OCD about...' No! No! No! You may think you are empathising or relating to others, but you're not. These are neurological conditions that nobody has a choice over; yes, they are spectrum based and vary in 'intensity' but those who are neurodivergent, or neurodiverse can't just turn it on and off like you or me! (Assuming you, too, are neurotypical!)

Whenever a student is identified by their primary area of need, the reason of identification is to help inform actions the school needs to put in place, not to fit a student simply into a category. In reality, as mentioned, individual children often have needs that cut across all these areas and their needs.

Just before I get you to move on, notice English as an Additional Language (EAL) is NOT a SEND category of need. Students with EAL needs should not mindlessly be placed on the SEND register or be given 'SEND interventions'. For more support with EAL, check out the resources on the National Subject Association for EAL website.

NOTE IT DOWN

THINK OF YOUR CLASS(ES). ARE YOU CONFIDENT YOU KNOW YOUR STUDENTS' PRIMARY NEEDS? IF SO, WHAT ADAPTATIONS ARE YOU MAKING FOR THOSE STUDENTS? ORGANISE THE SPACE BELOW TO WRITE DOWN THE INITIALS OF YOUR STUDENTS AND ADD THEIR PRIMARY NEEDS FOLLOWED BY A STRATEGY YOU USE TO SUPPORT THEM.

WHAT WILL YOU TRY, REFINE OR DITCH BASED ON WHAT YOU HAVE READ SO FAR?

Initials of student	Primary need	Secondary need	What works well	What to avoid

CHAPTER 2
LOW-EFFORT, HIGH-IMPACT IDEAS

This chapter explores the ideas:

- Many students commonly face challenges in specific areas of learning
- Implementing low-effort, adaptive strategies can aid students in overcoming learning barriers
- As teachers, we possess the capacity to support all our students effectively

DIFFERING NEEDS

You scan over your class list, looking at all the various codes/labels that come attached to your students. You diligently inform yourself and your planner that you have seven students with a K code, two students with an EHCP and twelve students who are eligible for Pupil Premium. Of the nine students with SEND, six of those have a 'double disadvantage' as they have an entitlement to PP too. Oh yes, you also have one Child We Care For (CWCF) and you also have two students who have English as an Additional Language (EAL). Based on national averages, this isn't an unusual classroom formation.

So, what next? Well, I have long said that education is the best possible **intervention** we can provide to our students. We need to get them to have as many potential doors open as possible by helping them to achieve what is best for each of them. However, whilst ensuring we want our students to succeed educationally, we need to be able to challenge what is now seen as the acceptable societal norm of what actually constitutes 'success.' I wrote about this years ago, but I will say it again – the modal reflection of SATs/GCSE attainment does not apply to everybody. Simply by logic alone one can see that. However, we all need to get accustomed to the fact that sometimes for some of our students getting a grade 1, or 3, or a scaled score of 92 is their best possible achievement and if it sets them up for their next step then we should celebrate this as much as a student getting 9 Grade 9s or SAT scores of 120!

We ALL want students learning; that's why you picked this book up I would imagine. And now I am here telling you the best intervention is to get them to learn. I will go on to say that mainly, to motivate a student, they need to feel/experience/taste success, which in turn creates a yearning for more success! If we get our students succeeding, it will encourage a want for more success. So how successful are you in ensuring your students are successful!? In most cases we have an uphill struggle because habitual failure or learned helplessness of both us and the students has set in due to unreasonable expectations of the notion of success. You may even claim apathy from your students and a complete disregard of wanting to try is the biggest stumbling block to some of them making progress. Well, let's place ourselves in their shoes for a minute – imagine going somewhere, daily, for hours on end, where all you feel is failure, or confusion or a feeling that this place isn't for you. As adults, we don't allow ourselves to feel like this for too long, but children, in many scenarios, are powerless. It may be that they present their feelings through refusal, but all behaviour is a form of some type of communication, and this is often a cry for help, and we should respond to it as such.

MAXIMUM OUTPUT

'Isaac, that's a wonderful sentence you have written there. You have used a metaphor extremely well and it's really painting a vivid picture for me in my mind'.

That statement is demonstrating the same level of effort as the following statement:

'Zakariya, the way your hyperbolic first paragraph foreshadows the impending doom thus inviting the reader into speculating what may occur next is riveting. I particularly like your one-word sentence. It really adds to the tension being built up.'

Why? How? Because both students are working to their maximum output. They are both trying their hardest. Do we as educators notice when a student is trying their hardest? Do you have the right level of modelled, taught, and shared expectations for your students?

What does 'Maximum output' for each of your students look like? Is it the same? Can it be the same? Do you know? Maximum output does not mean burning your students out like an overused tractor, but instead getting them to do as much as they are cognitively capable of, and not confusing being busy with seemingly working hard. Maximum output is stretching your students to the precipice of making a mistake, that sweet spot, where learning takes place, those eureka or light bulb moments. (Some might call it the Zone of Proximal Development – Vygotsky, 1978: 86.)

 REFLECTION

Think about the praise you offer to individual students. Are you as good at offering praise to students who may be finding the work challenging as you are with the students who are meeting or exceeding expectations? Think about ways that you can encourage students who are working at a range of levels.

I have mentioned the point about getting students feeling successful and that being probably the best way to motivate them, but **'HOW?'** is what I hear you whispering in a thundering voice. Well, let me tell you. I will now share four areas that students generally struggle with (I know there are many more barriers to learning, but I like to talk about these four as they are controllable items we can put in place to overcome some of these difficulties. There are of course uncontrollable areas, but surprisingly fewer than we might like to admit/acknowledge).

From these 'main' barriers I will provide you with some low-effort, high-impact strategies that you can put in place to support your students. These are quite generalist strategies, so you must be prepared to contextualise and refine for your students, which will hopefully make them feel more successful and therefore want more success from your lessons.

Let's get back to visualising our classes, our students, our children. We are noticing they are struggling with one or more of these difficulties:

1.   Reading/decoding

2.   Listening/comprehending

3.   Writing

4.   Time management

It is vital to remember that these areas of difficulties branch across all of the four main areas of needs which I mentioned in Chapter 1. These barriers are the expected mechanisms needed to learn in most schools for our students/ pupils/learners (it's fascinating how many different ways we have to refer to our children isn't it?).

It is also vital to stress here, again, that the above areas of need are not a hierarchical or exhaustive list – it is a list of areas where I feel we, as professional learners, can do some of that reasonable adjusting I was talking about. Or if you would prefer, these barriers are areas that you can adapt your lessons to.

READING AND DECODING

Ok, so what do we do? Let's tackle these barriers one at a time, reading/ decoding first. Reading is difficult – accessing texts is problematic for some, understanding and recalling what has just been read out may also be limited to some too. Before we think about reading, we need to consider whether the text we are presenting is readable. Because if we can't even see or make out what we are to read, we won't get anywhere fast!

The British Dyslexia Association has published a Readability Report that you can find on their website. This report provides us with clear guidelines of how to ensure we can make text/visuals we are using readable. **Wait**, 'but Amjad, I don't teach any dyslexic students'. Guess what colleagues, this is the best thing about most if not all SEND strategies, they can be **needed for some, but benefit all!** So, it's irrelevant whether you teach dyslexic students or not, these strategies will not be a detriment to any of your learners. Trust me, I ask colleagues in my training/CPD days, I show examples of what a bad strategy looks like and then show them what a good one looks like, and the contrast is vast and the accessibility for SEND and non-SEND colleagues is almost identical. (A little primary school reference there, I hope you got it people!)

Here are some strategies for you to use to help students struggling with elements of reading and decoding.

✎ IDEAS FOR THE CLASSROOM

1. *Pre-teach 'difficult' vocabulary.* Pre-teaching is the concept of teaching our students the vocabulary, skills or insights needed to access the upcoming lessons. Ascertain which vocabulary is needed for the effective understanding of the topics you are teaching and then ensure students use these in context, in advance. By doing this, we allow our students to NOT feel excluded from the lesson, or feel like the lesson is not for them, and therefore they can experience that feeling of success.

2. *Use visuals to reinforce understanding of Tier 1/2/3 words.* Visuals are handy and dual coding as a concept is extremely useful but remember one simple rule of thumb – when using a visual, make reference to it and do not assume all the students know why that visual was chosen! P.S. I am a big fan of standardised PowerPoints; for support with this please go to the Try This Teaching website: www.TryThisTeaching.com

3. *Chunk and sequence.* Break text into chunks and space lines out. Chunking text and sequencing information is not any more difficult than the current formatting options we use; it just might not be what you're used to doing.

4. *Use ruler line guides* to help focus words on the extracts/texts. By making this a whole class strategy you are not 'differentiating' but just ensuring all students can benefit. Get partners to track where the reader currently is. This enables them both to remain focussed.

5. Consider a student's *reading age* with the extracts/texts you are using. But how? Do you understand what these differing

reading ages mean? This is a potential whole CPD session – what use are reading ages if we do not know what to do with them, or more importantly, what not to do with them?

6. Use *highlighters* to get students to highlight words they DO NOT know rather than what they imagine to be important. Make the parameters of what 'they don't know' clear, i.e., they are not able to use the word in a sentence or explain what the word means to others. The highlighted information then gives you details on what further pre-teaching or re-teaching of key information you have to do.

7. *Avoid underlining* words in your PowerPoints as it often affects the readability of words, especially when you are using letters such as g, y, or p. Here is this sentence again, underlined – notice the difference? <u>Avoid underlining words in your PowerPoints as it often affects the readability of words, especially when you are using letters such as g, y, or p.</u>

REFLECTION

Search the tools below by using the information in the Website/tool column and then jot down what you will try and refine.

Website/tool	Description	What will you Try/ Refine?
Lexile Analyzer	Measures text complexity and provides a Lexile measure	

(Continued)

(Continued)

Website/tool	Description	What will you Try/ Refine?
Built-in tools (e.g., Microsoft Word, Google Docs)	Check readability using Flesch-Kincaid and similar tests	
TextEvaluator	Analyses text for readability, providing scores and tips	
Readable	Offers readability scores and suggestions for improvement	
Online-Utility.org	Provides various readability formulas for text analysis	
Newsela	Provides news articles at various reading levels	
CommonLit	Offers texts with associated reading levels for educators	

These tools can assist in estimating the reading level of a text or extract, which can be useful for selecting appropriate materials for students with varying reading abilities.

IDEAS FOR THE CLASSROOM

Try, Refine, Ditch – **you have not read those words for a while now, right? So here they are, back! What will you Try, Refine and Ditch to help students with the difficulties we discussed above? I have given you *some* examples to help!**

READING/DECODING

Try	Refine	Ditch
Experiment with different visuals for PowerPoints	Fine-tune the most effective reading strategies	
	Optimise the use of assistive technology for better results	
Set a routine for use of a ruler line guide in lessons		

LISTENING/COMPREHENDING

'Sammi! Did you hear what I said?'

'Timmy, are you listening?'

'Rosie, how many times have I told you to do your work?'

'Alina, why aren't you doing your work?!'

This progression of questioning might look familiar to you. These might seem like questions posed to an inattentive student or somebody simply not listening; however, you might also be directing them at somebody struggling with listening and comprehending what is being said. Rather than drawing attention to these students and assuming the worst, here are some low-effort, high-impact suggestions for what you can do to support them.

IDEAS FOR THE CLASSROOM

1. Again, *pre-teach difficult vocabulary* but in particular words that are linked to particular instructions: 'Ok, everybody,

(Continued)

I need you to face the front and *focus* on me'. Have we assumed the word focus is fully understood and known? Have you modelled, repeated and reminded what that should look like? How often?

2. How about giving students time to *discuss* answers before asking for feedback. A simple strategy you can use for this is 'Think, Pair, Share'. For example, 'What is the best possible solution to avoid this happening? Partner A turn and talk to Partner B and talk through what you think, by asking them...I will then ask for feedback in 45 seconds' (timer clearly displayed on the board). Ensure you explain what the Think element includes, what the Pair element means and then how you will Share. Don't just expect expectations, teach them, model them, and then repeat them.

3. If you are a teacher who needs students to listen to some recorded information, pourquoi?! Well, you can help students achieve their maximum output by giving students a *transcript* of the recording/sound/listening.

4. You could also simply add *subtitles/closed captions* to your videos when playing, and/or use the speed function from YouTube to slow videos down, or speed them up (I wish this function were available to some adults too, right?!) Remember, don't click on the subtitles option when there are already auto-generated captions. And fight the temptation to give in to your students who will say they don't like the subtitles. They usually don't like them because they have to work harder, but if it results in cognitive overload, then you make that call.

5. And finally, remember if a student didn't understand what you asked them to do, don't just say it again S L O W E R R R R... *say it again, but in a different format/way*. Say it so they understand it, not in a way that you think they

SHOULD understand. Oh, I forgot to mention, make sure you sequence your instructions, so you don't add something on at the end. The irony.

6. Be clear, have signals and establish routines to instil good listening skills. It is easier to *repeat/remind than to get upset that somebody has forgotten*!

Now, complete your Try, Refine and Ditch lists. I have given you *some* more examples below to help, again.

LISTENING/COMPREHENDING

Try	Refine	Ditch
Implement active listening techniques as part of your class routines		Stop using passive listening methods
	Improve active listening skills through practice	
Utilise closed captioning or transcripts for audio content		Eliminate audio content without accessibility features

WRITING

Next challenge – writing. Students can't, won't, don't write? Firstly, we need to understand writing is both a physical action and a mental one. Therefore, we need to create the correct physical environment to aid effective writing. Where are the students sitting, what are they sitting on, what pencil/pen are they using, how far back from the table, how close to the table, where is their back in relation to the chair, do their feet touch the ground and finally, who are they sitting next to? All these factors affect the physical act of writing; you are in control of these factors, so adapt and change them to create better outcomes. Oh, sorry, I didn't explain exactly what would be most beneficial and to whom. In actual fact, I intentionally didn't sequence or chunk this information very well, did I? But why have I let this go to print like this? Well, something you should also be aware of is that **NON-EXAMPLES** also support one's learning process. Showing somebody what is **not** correct and is in fact a misconception, or is wrong, helps support the correct version; this is in addition to showing students a modelled correct answer too.

Ok, let us start that explanation again. To support the physical act of writing ensure your students are sitting with their backs against their chair, that they are not being affected by their partner/neighbour who may write with the opposite hand from them, for example. Students should also be able to rest their feet on the floor; if they aren't able to do this you might want to consider using a wobble board.

We need to also consider their desk. Could a writing slope be beneficial? I won't go into the mechanics of this too much here, as this is just a Little Guide, but have a think… . The Driver Youth Trust has some useful videos on YouTube demonstrating an optimal writing position. I suggest getting students to break their bad seating habits as soon as possible because it's physically uncomfortable for their bodies. Despite the pleas, leaning back, heads on elbows, writing with straight legs, is not optimal. The transitional nature of moving from our listening positions to our writing positions signifies the next activity to be completed.

Here is how we can do this with precision and intentionality.

1. Everybody place your pens down, close your books and (turn fully) to face the front, looking at me, if you can.

2. Ok class, we are now going to do some writing.

3. Can everybody get into our writing positions we have rehearsed previously.

4. If you can't remember, look at what others and I am doing.

Now that everybody is comfortable, we'll move onto some effective writing. Let's work on this first portion together. With this **narration** of learning I am signposting what I want my students to do with the utmost clarity.

1.   Once I have their full mental and physical attention, I will narrate a model, whilst visually displaying what I am writing, and why I am writing it.

2.   I will 'talk the walk' so to speak, asking probing questions whilst doing so. Talk the walk – a phrase I'm borrowing from a colleague on Twitter – is the idea that you talk through what exactly you are writing, why, when and where. It is about talking about the journey in vivid detail.

3.   I will then get students to copy down my model/example.

The I do, we do, you do model becomes more like I do, we do, we do, I do, I do, we do, I do, we do, I do, we do, we do, I do, I do, now **you** do (for more information on this model, see Evidence-Based Teaching, 2023).

So we have modelled and we now need to make sure we don't hinder our students' writing in any way, for example by stipulating how much they have to physically write. Instead say how much they **could** write, e.g. instead of saying 'I would like you to write half a page', I would say, 'I need everybody to write three paragraphs'. This is also automatic differentiation because remember, I want everybody's maximum output, but this may well of course be different! There are lots of other strategies we can use to support students with writing, but I don't want to overload you, because, you know, I am treating this book much like a lesson of mine.

In the classroom, teachers often act as judges, where legibility is sometimes mistaken for intelligence, and penmanship is misinterpreted as potential.
Amjad Ali

Please do not conflate neatness of writing with hard work or extra effort. We as adults are extremely biased and our bias towards handwriting is confusing and illogical, but all biases are, right? We seem to think those who write beautifully are 'lovely' children, but those who write messily are not working or trying as hard. (Personal memories flooding back here!)

 IDEAS FOR THE CLASSROOM

Try, Refine and Ditch again, to help students with this difficulty. I have given you *more* examples to help!

WRITING

Try	Refine	Ditch
		Avoid mentioning an amount of physical space one should take when completing a writing task
	Fine-tune time management strategies	
Experiment with time management timers for writing tasks		

TIME

Finally, you may have students who struggle to finish tasks in the time you have set them; they never seem to complete their work in the time allocated and they always seem to need more time to fully complete their expected outcomes. Well, assuming they are all working diligently and still not able to finish, I am sorry to say, it's probably not their fault they're not finishing, but yours! (What?!) Yes, yours – you need to allocate time to tasks better and be clearer about the reason. For example, 'I need you to complete these three questions; I will give you 10 minutes per question. That will allow you to read the question, then re-read the extract and finally write your answers down. That means you have 30 minutes to complete this task'.

If you are finding that your students are still struggling with time management, then help them manage their time. Allocate timers – these may need to be physical timers, sand timers for example, or digital, or virtual, or a countdown timer on the board. Try not to make these too abstract or distracting by having silly sounds attached to them.

Don't forget, when posing questions or giving instructions, allow for thinking time, or processing time too. Teachers are notoriously bad at pouncing on the first hand that goes up, or they worry excessively if a hand has not gone up immediately. Break that habit, now!

Are you aware of what the term 'executive functioning skills' refers to? Are you aware that some of the 'gaps' many of our students display may be a skill they are yet to develop, or finesse? Or potentially due to a child's SEND needs, a skill they will be unable to grasp fully? These executive functioning skills are critical for students to be successful in both academic and non-academic aspects of school life. Children with well-developed executive functioning skills tend to be more organised, capable of self-regulation, and better equipped to handle the demands of the school environment. Teachers, parents and educators can support the development of these skills through various strategies and interventions to help children reach their full academic potential.

Here is my hunch: most, if not all, problems that occur with learning in classrooms happen when one or more executive functioning skill has not been catered for. Have a think, reflect on your own experiences in the classroom as you review the table below, which outlines some ideas about what you can do to help.

Executive functioning skill	Relevance in school	What teachers can do to help
Self-control	Following instructions from teachers	Provide clear and concise instructions
	Resisting distractions during lessons	Minimise classroom distractions
		Teach self-regulation techniques
Cognitive flexibility	Adapting to different subjects or activities	Encourage discussions that explore multiple perspectives
	Problem-solving when faced with challenges	Assign tasks that require flexibility and adaptability
Working memory	Remembering and applying instructions	Break down complex tasks into smaller steps
	Mental maths in class	Use mnemonic devices and memory aids
Planning and organisation	Homework and project planning	Teach organisational strategies
	Organising school materials	Provide assignment calendars and due dates
		Offer checklists and reminders
Task initiation	Starting homework and tasks promptly	Set clear expectations and deadlines
	Initiating long-term projects	Help students break tasks into manageable chunks, sequenced
Emotional regulation	Managing frustration and emotions during learning	Foster a supportive and emotionally safe classroom environment
	Handling social interactions	Teach emotional self-regulation techniques

Executive functioning skill	Relevance in school	What teachers can do to help
Self-monitoring	Self-assessment of work and progress	Encourage self-reflection and self-assessment
	Staying on track during assignments	Provide feedback and guidance for self-monitoring
Time management	Meeting assignment and project deadlines	Teach time management techniques and strategies
	Managing class schedules	Create a consistent daily routine and schedule
Goal setting	Setting academic and long-term goals	Help students set SMART (Specific, Measurable, Achievable, Relevant, Time-bound) goals
	Planning for educational and career objectives	Discuss career aspirations

Teachers play a crucial role in nurturing these executive functioning skills in students by creating an environment that supports their development and by providing guidance, strategies and resources to help students enhance all of these skills.

HINTS AND TIPS

Pace and time management are two elements of teaching that we seldom get right. We can be criticised for not enough pace, and in the same breath told that we are not taking long enough with certain instructions. The trick is to ensure that we set clear parameters around the tasks that we want our students to do. Don't forget, if your students are entitled to extra time in assessments and examinations, this should be considered when setting in-class tasks too!

Visit the Joint Council for Qualifications website for more information about Exams Access Arrangements (JCQ, n.d.).

✐ IDEAS FOR THE CLASSROOM

Try, Refine and Ditch to help students with this difficulty. I have given you *some* more examples to help!

TIME

Try	Refine	Ditch
Set specific time blocks for focused work and quantify why time is being allocated		
Try using timers or Pomodoro technique for productivity		Stop investing time in low-priority tasks that offer little value
	Refine timer-based productivity methods	

NOTE IT DOWN

Split this page into four sections with the headings:

1. Reading/decoding
2. Listening/comprehending
3. Writing
4. Time

Come back to this page in 1-4 weeks, now jot down 'What difference did your adaptations make?'

CHAPTER 3
UNDER- AND OVER-REPRESENTATION

This chapter explores the ideas:

- The diagnosis of SEND needs may be influenced by assumptions and biases
- It is crucial to investigate the over- and under-representation in various SEND areas
- Being mindful of the intersectional connections between SEND and race is essential

There are a multitude of contextual, cultural, and religious issues, barriers and misconceptions which affect, and hinder the way ethnic minorities, or marginalised groups experience the provision of Special Educational Needs in schools in the UK. The best thing about inclusion though, is that if we support the minority, it will of course potentially help everybody. (Needed for some but benefits all.) Yet, the same people arguing for bespoke, individualised, personalised support are the ones forgetting about the differences between perceptions and perspectives with SEND from some particular communities.

The esteemed organisation, Special Needs Jungle, tells us that:

> Acknowledging intersectionality in SEND illustrates how multiple modes of advantage, and disadvantage, discrimination, and privilege, affect children's access to services. These factors also impact a family's ability to advocate for their child. This intersection is fundamental in predicting outcomes for children. When you consider we have a SEND system that already fails children who are otherwise advantaged, it is easy to see how those at the margins lose out even further. (Special Needs Jungle, 2022: p. 2)

I read this and cheered at how clear this statement is, yet it feels as though this is something which isn't always embodied within the education sector.

Here are some pieces of research for you to gain some clarity and further information around these issues:

1.   *Ethnic disproportionality in the identification of Special Educational Needs (SEN) in England: Extent, causes and consequences.* An exploration of 12 years of data trends along with two longitudinal analyses of 500,000 pupils (Strand and Lindorff, 2018).

     As I am all about saving teachers time, I have provided a little distillation of this research for you here...

     •   Persistent concerns over the disproportionate representation of ethnic minority groups in special education in England.

- Extensive research reveals Black pupils are more likely to be identified with Special Educational Needs (SEND), particularly for 'Intellectual Disabilities and Emotional Disturbance'.

- Under-representation also exists, as seen with Asian pupils with Autism Spectrum Disorders (ASD).

- Identification with SEND can have both positive and negative outcomes.

- Comprehensive research using contemporary data aims to understand and address ethnic disproportionality in England, as prior studies had methodological limitations.

2. *Special Educational Needs and Ethnicity: Issues of Over- and Under- Representation.* This piece of research completed at the University of Warwick looks at the relevant pupil census data and dives into a robust literature review of US and the UK (Lindsay et al., 2006).

   Here is a little summary:

   - Socio-economic disadvantage and gender have stronger associations than ethnicity with the prevalence of Special Educational Needs (SEN) and some SEN categories.

   - Under-representation of different minority ethnic groups compared to White British pupils still exists in various SEN categories.

   - Black Caribbean and Mixed White and Black Caribbean pupils are about 1.5 times more likely to be identified with Behavioural, Emotional and Social Difficulties (BESD).

   - Bangladeshi pupils are nearly twice as likely to have a hearing impairment, and Pakistani pupils are 2–2.5 times more likely to have certain SEN.

   - Asian and Chinese pupils are less likely to be identified with certain SEN, possibly due to challenges in distinguishing learning difficulties from issues related to English as an Additional Language (EAL).

- Travellers of Irish Heritage and Gypsy/Roma pupils are over-represented in various SEN categories, with factors ranging from negative teacher attitudes to mobility and dropout issues.

3. *Intersectionality in SEND: Families experiences in Schools.* SNJ Intersectionality Panel members and Council for Disabled Children dive into the issues, concepts and values of intersectionality and SEND (Special Needs Jungle, 2022).

A brief summary:

- Educators should ask uncomfortable questions and include marginalised communities in policy development.

- Understanding students' behaviours requires considering their diverse perspectives.

- Schools should assess whether they are welcoming and accessible to all families.

- Subtle racism continues despite decreasing priority in teacher training and schools.

- 'Colour blindness' can diminish the value of diversity, and inclusive policies should align with the experiences of marginalised communities.

Do not forget that the revered Swann Report argued that 'multicultural understanding must permeate all aspects of a school's work – it is not a separate topic that can be welded on to existing practices' (1985: p. 288).

 **REFLECTION**

Why do you think some children might be over-represented when it comes to different areas of SEND? Can you reflect on why the Swann Report stated this and how it helps us as teachers to have a multicultural understanding of our pupils?

The quote from the Swann Report was published in 1985. However, we have not seen much change in this area, have we? As we now know, we must be more aware of this issue because as government data shows (GOV.UK, 2023a), the percentage of pupils from minority ethnic backgrounds is 35.7% across all school types, continuing a trend of increases in recent years (34.5% in 2021/22). The percentage varies by school type:

- 36.1% in primary schools (up from 34.8% in 2020/21)

- 35.4% in secondary schools (up from 34.1%)

- 31.3% in special schools (up from 31.0%)

- 25.4% in AP schools (up from 25.1%)

These figures do not include those where ethnicity is unclassified.

So, let's be realistic, it is of utmost importance that we understand the intersectional elements at play with our students. It is important to stress that all of the above terms are 'man-made' and are designed to group individuals into identifiable factions, or as I like to say, into gangs. Why gangs? Because, it has a negative connotation and I think grouping people in general, through no power of their own, is negative. As you would imagine, or indeed have experienced, with anything socially constructed it is able to be misused, and bias, prejudice, discrimination and therefore microaggressions can and will creep in through having preconceived ideas about groups.

Reflection

These uncomfortable questions must be answered. It is our job to seek clarity of our young people's issues and without acknowledging the barriers we will not be able to do this.

Have a go at answering these questions.

1. **Do you have children from Traveller backgrounds? Are they more likely to feature on your SEND register relative to other backgrounds?**

2. **Which South Asian country is least likely to feature on your SEND register? Pakistan? Bangladesh or India? Why?**

(Continued)

3.   Are those same students more likely to feature on other SEND specific needs?

4.   What's the ratio of Black, Caribbean boys on your SEND register compared to White?

5.   Which racial group is most suspended or excluded from your school? Are they less likely to be identified with a SEMH need? Or are they just, you know, angrier, more aggressive? (Hint – the answer is no, they are not!)

6.   Are you involving marginalised voices in your policies and documentation?

7.   How much interaction and engagement are you getting from ethnic minority or marginalised groups? How have you measured this?

ASSUMPTIONS

Returning to your SEND register, is there **under**- or **over**-representation in certain needs? Are you comfortable with some of the assumptions you may be making towards students and their backgrounds? Are you able to include all families for example? How? Are you as a SENDCO/ is your SENDCO the gatekeeper of all this? Please note that accepting, acknowledging and noticing your biases is different from preventing and dismantling the damage they create. To support your students best you need to work on dismantling your biases and bringing in positive action that supports all.

PARENT/CARER VOICE

Over the years of working closely with all different types of families and carers I have had many forms of feedback. Parents, carers, siblings, relatives, family friends and many others have made comments about the lack of any real understanding from schools around cultural expectations in different ethnic and racial groups. I have also been told about the unnecessary and false assumptions of, for example, Muslim families unlikely to want to accept any additional needs due to stigma and social isolation. I have also had conversations whilst supporting families around some members of ethnic minority communities feeling as if they need their husband (a man) with them for their meetings, or maybe even they will only be listened to if they are dressed in 'westernised clothing'. Finally, amongst many comments which were also echoed in The Special Needs Jungle's Survey in 2022 was that families from many African families feel as if they have not been approached in regard to SEND due to the stereotype that SEND is not accepted in those communities.

What do your families say to you? Or dare I say, about your provision?

IDEAS FOR YOUR CLASSROOM

Have you gathered a student/parent/carer voice yet?

Whatever you do, you must vary the way you seek to collect data ... How?

- Send an online questionnaire.

- Get families to complete a paper version of your questionnaire too.

- Do you have translated versions of your documents/communication for parents who may not speak English? There are professional services you can use, or try Google Translate.

- You could offer SEND 'coffee' mornings/evenings to have face-to-face time with parents.

 REFLECTION

Think about how you will make a conscious change to your current practices. Here are some suggestions you could work through:

1.   Equality, Diversity and Inclusion training.

2.   Involvement of marginalised groups in key events such as parent/carer evenings, review meetings, etc.

3.   Audit of current provision and numbers from which groups identify.

   a.   What is the problem? How do we break it down into smaller/actionable issues?

   b.   Who is responsible for the issue we want to address? In fact, is there someone responsible?

   c.   What are the barriers we need to overcome? Are they financial, ideological, logistical, physical? What are the facilitating forces that need to be added to ensure things move forward (e.g., a new role/team/working party needs to be created, a new budget needs to be allocated, a new policy needs to be written up, etc.)?

   d.   Where do we want to be in 2 years? 1 year? 6 months? 3 months? What steps do we need to take to get there?

   e.   Include celebration events after key milestones have been reached.

The following table is an example of an action plan to put these points into motion.

Issue	Responsible person	Barriers to overcome	Facilitating forces	Timeframe	Celebration events
a) Problem identification					
Identify the lack of representation and support for students from Traveller backgrounds within the SEND register	SEND Coordinator	Break down the problem by gathering data, e.g., number of Traveller students, their specific SEND needs	Budget allocation for additional support	2 weeks to complete data collection	Data collection milestone
b) Responsibility clarification					
Determine if there is a designated person responsible for addressing the issue and clarify their role	School leadership	Check existing roles and responsibilities to ensure someone is accountable for Traveller student support within the SEND register	Create a specific role if needed	1 month for role clarification	Role clarification achievement
c) Barriers and facilitating forces					
Identify barriers such as financial constraints and create facilitating forces like budget allocation	HT/finance department	Budget allocation and resource allocation	Budget allocation and policy development	Ongoing budget allocation	Remaining within budget

(Continued)

(Continued)

Issue	Responsible person	Barriers to overcome	Facilitating forces	Timeframe	Celebration events
d) Goal setting and steps					
Set goals:					
2 years – improve the representation of Traveller students in the SEND register	SEND coordinator/ school leadership	Create tailored support programs	Budget allocation, policy development	Ongoing throughout the timeframes	Milestones for each goal
1 year – implement tailored support programs		Develop a policy for inclusive education			
6 months – develop a policy for inclusive education		Collect data on the specific needs of Traveller students			
3 months – identify specific needs of Traveller students					
e) Celebration events					
Recognise achievements at key milestones	SEND coordinator/ school leadership	Celebrate achievements at the completion of each major step in the plan, e.g., successful policy development or support program implementation	Internal recognition and awards	At each major milestone	Milestone celebration events

Source: Citizen School, 2020

This action plan outlines the problem, identifies responsibilities, highlights barriers and facilitating forces, sets specific goals with time frames, and incorporates celebrations after achieving key milestones. It focuses on addressing the lack of support for students from Traveller backgrounds within the SEND register.

In case you are thinking, well there are not so many practical strategies in this chapter, the reason for this is that I wanted to spend time encouraging you to **reflect** on your practices and assumptions and biases to support you in seeing where you might need to address a gap in learning, or think about how you can be part of positive action within your school.

Here is a tip for you: when reflecting, make sure you remember that we reflect by looking in a mirror, by looking at ourselves. We don't reflect by looking through a window at others; that's comparison. Be the best version of you that you can be by noticing what you should do differently, what you shouldn't do anymore, and what else you could do instead.

Please do not get distracted by terms such as 'woke' – working on these areas is about being just, being equitable and ensuring everybody, no matter which gang you were thrust into, gets a fairer shot at life.

NOTE IT DOWN

USE THE FOLLOWING TABLE TO POPULATE FIGURES BASED ON YOUR COHORT, RE-READ THE ABOVE INFORMATION, AND WORK OUT YOUR ACTION PLAN. WHERE I HAVE LEFT SPACE AT THE END OF THE TABLE, YOU PICK THE AREA YOU WANT TO INVESTIGATE FURTHER.

Primary need	PP/ FSM	EAL	Race	Nationality	Gender	SEND- K	SEND- E	Other Info:
Autism								
ADHD								
Dyslexia								
PD								
SEMH								

CHAPTER 4
NEURODIVERSITY/ NEURODIVERGENCE

This chapter explores the ideas:

- Neurodiversity/neurodivergence refers to the range of neurological conditions people may have
- There are some generalist strategies available to support individuals with these neurological conditions

NEURODIVERSITY

It is important to note that I can't write this chapter from a platform of lived experience. I can't write this from understanding physically, mentally and emotionally what it is like being neurodiverse or neurodivergent. I am what one would refer to as someone who has an absence of a neurological condition such as autism, dyslexia or ADHD, as neurotypical.

So, with this out in the open and clear, how can I then write a chapter in this book about ways to support students with these needs? Well, 18+ years of teaching experience with students with these diverse needs every single year of my teaching career has enabled me to create a toolkit of low-effort, high-impact strategies that support students with their learning and regulation.

I also make it my personal job to read, learn, talk, find out, synthesise research, evaluate pedagogy and hone the suggestions of others. It is quite literally my job, as I deliver CPD in this area and have done for the past eight years, alongside working four days a week as a senior leader, SENDCO, inclusion lead and raising standards lead.

I have used a multitude of sources to generate suggestions, advice and guidance to support students. Now, remember, you need to apply these generalist strategies in the context of your young people's needs and the students you have in front of you. It might be that some of these suggestions don't work and if that's the case, chuck it out and try something new. Always invite the student you are working with to be a collaborator when you try out different strategies, ask them for feedback on the strategy and whether they want to make tweaks. It's also important to get feedback on yourself. This may be quite fear inducing, but it's important to know if there is anything your students might need you to change to support them better.

For each of the three core areas of need that students generally struggle with in classroom settings I have used their respective 'subject association'. For autism, I have referred to the National Autistic Society, for dyslexia, The British Dyslexia Association and for ADHD, The ADHD Foundation. (I will be giving more details on these and other key websites you can source information from in my penultimate chapter!). Right, let's get started.

AUTISM

KEY INFORMATION

- 700,000 + people are living with this lifelong condition in the UK.

- Only around 16% of autistic adults are in full-time employment.

- Some learning difficulties are interconnected with autism, but it does not automatically mean a delay in academic ability.

- Autistic people may see, hear and feel differently from others.

So, let's begin. How cluttered is your classroom? How busy is it? Is it distracting? Well, sit at the back of your classroom, on the far left chair, and look up and out towards where you normally stand to teach. Many autistic students will experience sensory overload from extremely busy, noisy and cluttered spaces. Could you help reduce this? Yes? Then do it! Studies do show that the effect of distraction does reduce over time, as it becomes normalised, but why let students have to 'fight' their way to being OK?

Routines and processes are a key component to efficient and effective teaching. Autistic students benefit from having clear routines, structures and parameters (in fact, most people do, right?). Visual timetables are therefore extremely useful. But my top tip for you would be to invest some real time in working through with your young people what happens if the usual routine can't be fulfilled. The strategies (support with executive functioning skills) to deal with change are ones you will benefit from having.

Visual and tactile support for autistic students are useful strategies to turn abstract concepts into concrete representations; do you have physical, tangible resources to emphasise key classroom activities, behaviours and expectations?

As I mentioned, autistic students may see, hear and feel things differently from me, and potentially some of you reading this book right now, so a strategy we all need to learn is to help get our students to recognise their emotions. They can do this by using a stress scale such as the one adapted in the following table.

Stress point	How I am feeling
5	Incredibly angry, I can't cope
4	I am beginning to get very angry
3	I do not like this position I am in right now
2	Feeling OK
1	All is good

You can use this scale by making your own copy, printing, laminating and providing it to your students to indicate where they are. If you do use this scale, the time you invest in explaining how to use the scale, what the numbers reflect and how to recognise feelings will really pay off. Do this rather than simply handing it to a young person to use when they are getting angry.

HINTS AND TIPS

Here is some advice I can offer you too. NEVER ever, anymore, refer to a student as being challenging, or difficult, or having a 'meltdown' or 'kicking off'. Instead, when they are on stress scale point five, refer to them as a distressed or dysregulated child/ student/young person. This subtle change in language will help with your own self-regulation and help you to better support your students when they are facing a challenging situation.

REPAIR AND RESTORE

Repairing, resetting and restoring relationships is vital in every aspect of life. Autistic students may find it more difficult to acknowledge a fault or problem, so the use of 'Social Stories' or 'Comic Strip Conversations' can really benefit some of your young people (Carol Gray – Social Stories, 2024). Social Stories involve talking through the issues and addressing where others may have felt emotions unbeknown to the young person at the time; this is similar to Comic Strip Conversations as they also allow for the physical interpretation of what has happened.

Look at the following table – the 'What can be done' column is adapted from **Milestones Autism Planning resources** (Milestones Autism Resources, 2024). They have included in their stress scale what to do in that situation. This should be personalised and bespoke for your children.

Stress point	How I am feeling	What can be done
5	Very angry, I can't cope	I need to leave this space
		I need to go to my safe space
		I may need to be alone
4	I am beginning to get very angry	I need a quick break
		I may need to find somebody I trust to speak to
		I may need to write down how I am feeling
3	I do not like this position I am in right now	I need to say this is 'hard/I am struggling'
2	Feeling OK	I need to keep focusing
		I need to use breathing techniques
1	All is good, nothing is bothering me	I need feedback

You could also think about completing a De-escalation Plan – or wait, is it called a Consistent Support Plan, or no, it's a Pastoral Support Plan, no it's an Individual Education Plan! Look, whatever title you use, the aim is to list out, with robust communication with the young person, trusted adults and parents/carers, any of the student's triggers, what escalation looks like so you can intervene before it gets too far and how to repair and restore.

All students, but particularly autistic students, need careful communication, which is clear, accurate and simplified. It should be given in manageable chunks and reinforced visually where possible. Where students display weak organisational skills, then practise, rehearse and repeat how to become better, provide both visual and physical timers, prompt scripts, and written and verbal reminders. (Remember, help with those executive functioning skills we might take for granted.)

DYSLEXIA

As mentioned in Chapter 1, dyslexia is a SpLD – can you remember what this stands for? The amalgamation of the Greek and English words of difficulty and speech enables us to only understand part of the difficulties dyslexic people experience.

Some characteristics and difficulties that people with SpLDs face with some suggestions of what you can do to support them are given in the following table.

Difficulty	How to support
Memory	Use mnemonics and repetition
	Provide visual aids and memory aids (notes, reminders)
Organisation	Teach organisational strategies
	Use visual schedules and checklists
	Break tasks into smaller steps
Writing	Provide assistive technology (spell-check, speech-to-text)
	Encourage graphic organisers
	Focus on content over spelling initially
Visual processing	Use visual aids and organisers
	Minimise visual clutter
	Provide dyslexia-friendly fonts and colour-coding

Difficulty	How to support
Auditory processing	Use clear language and concise instructions
	Provide visual cues alongside verbal information
	Allow extra processing time
Reading	Utilise multisensory reading programs
	Provide audiobooks and coloured overlays (if relevant)
	Focus on comprehension strategies
	Allow breaks during reading
Time management	Teach time management skills
	Use visual schedules and timers
	Break tasks into smaller time segments
	Provide clear expectations for deadlines
Concentration and focus	Minimise distractions in the environment
	Allow breaks and movement
	Use tools such as concentration tools to help maintain focus

A key area of dyslexia that you can have a direct impact on with minimal effort is the way you present information and resources to your student. The British Dyslexia Association's Style Guide report (British Dyslexia Association, n.d.), which you can find online, lays out firm, clear and effective guidance on what one should and should not do.

I won't patronise you and summarise those here for you, as it is just a case of looking at the suggestions; however, I want you to do this and add your notes below.

Decide which of the elements in the style guide report you will Try, Refine and Ditch from your current systems. At this point it is useful to tell you how to phase your changes throughout this book where you have written down your 'Tries, Refines and Ditches': you now need to go back and add an S, M or L next to each idea (S standing for Short, M for Medium and L for… you've guessed it, Long). These are to help you phase in your implementation intentions by identifying the time needed to assess each strategy. Taking things slowly and doing them well is much more effective than quick wins.

IDEAS FOR YOUR CLASSROOM

Some further manageable tweaks you should make to your teaching for dyslexic students is to ensure you do the following:

1. **Pause between giving instructions to allow for processing time.**

2. **Ask for repetition or check back, where the student(s) repeat back given instructions.**

3. **Use visuals to reinforce routines and structures.**

4. **Declutter, keep your desk, displays and area around your screens clutter free – this helps dyslexic students, autistic students, and students with ADHD!**

5. **Use technology! I am signposting items later on, remember.**

It is vital that I pause here for a second and remind everybody that these aren't exhaustive strategies and are not digging into needs deeply, but these are strategies that are designed to make SEND teaching more manageable and hopefully to support wins in the classroom as teachers need to feel as much success as the students, as success breeds more success.

ADHD

Let's now talk about ADHD. The ADHD Foundation shares this explanation of what it feels like to have ADHD, which I think is really helpful in dispelling this idea that anyone with ADHD should 'just CONCENTRATE more!'.

ADHD is like a TV set that isn't receiving a perfect signal. For the student, it's as if the channel keeps **changing**. **Imagine** you are watching the news on BBC1. Suddenly, somebody picks up the remote control and **flicks over** to ITV. A second later the **programme changes** to Channel 4 and then back to BBC1. **Then it switches** to BBC2. If you were asked about the news on BBC1 you might find it **hard to remember**. It's **difficult to focus** on one thing at a time because something new is always coming along (Shire, 2018: p. 14).

Ok, so what can we do to help/support and provide for our students who live with ADHD? Firstly, I would love for us all to reframe our perspectives on students with ADHD. Let's stop saying they get distracted easily, or distract others but instead say they are highly in tune with their surroundings and very observant! Or let's not automatically run to the sanction book if a student interrupts but see it as a desire to contribute.

 IDEAS FOR YOUR CLASSROOM

Here are some ideas to support students with ADHD:

1.   **When it comes to seating here are a few suggestions – you could sit them next to students that could support them (called Body Doubling) or you could seat them next to you, and always make sure your student is not seated next to any natural distractions.**

2.   **Provide them with extra time on tests/assignments if needed/approved.**

3.   **Make sure to use clear instructions; chunk and sequence them to make sure they are understandable. Check that the child understands before letting them go and try.**

4.   **Use eye contact, proximity to you and gestures to support redirection of attention and behaviours.**

(Continued)

5. Agree a personalised signal of warning that is not immediately obvious to others, for example, placing a highlighter on their desk indicates they are not doing what they should. When you remove the highlighter, it shows them that they are back on track.

6. Provide frequent and immediate feedback. A common lesson in the UK is around 60 minutes long; break this down into 15-minute chunks and provide regular, immediate feedback to them, their behaviours, attitude and work.

7. Use positive reinforcement.

8. Ensure there is a routine and a process for common actions, like getting books, pens, tidying away. Work through these in coordination with your students.

9. Ensure your language is clear and avoids conditional demands such as 'do _____ or _____ will/won't happen'. Instead try, 'Next item for us to complete is_____ so we can move on to_____. This will show me you have worked really hard'.

10. Use a stress scale with these students too. Allow for technology to be used to assist with tasks.

11. Allow for breaks, moving around and fidgeting – don't try to control these things! In fact, these adjustments are beneficial for a lot of students.

12. Offer additional help with staying organised.

13. Declutter! Make changes to the classroom to make sure it isn't full of distractions or anything that would create a sensory overload.

14. Don't let students say, 'I can't do this!' or 'I don't know what to do'. Instead get them into their routine of finishing the sentence, 'Help me with...' Try it, trust me!

Overall, the aim for supporting students with neurodivergence is to build esteem, success and relational improvements with you. Find out what they like, build on it, talk about it, but please do remember if you find out your young person likes trains, don't design every lesson around trains! You won't know what they are interested in until you interest them in it!

NOTE IT DOWN

I WILL LEAVE THIS SPACE FOR YOU TO NOTE DOWN YOUR THOUGHTS ABOUT THE FOLLOWING QUESTIONS.

Accommodations	Instructions	Interventions
What can you do to make learning more efficient and effective for your students?	How can you vary the way you ask your students to learn?	How can you head off difficulties in learning tasks?

CHAPTER 5
WORKING TOGETHER

This chapter explores the ideas:

- What the role of a SENDCO includes
- We are not alone in our pursuit of excellence for students with additional/differing learning needs
- We all need a helping hand being signposted in the right direction

SENDCO OR 'MENDCO'

'Where is the SENDCO?'

'Anybody seen the SENDCO?'

'I was waiting for the SENDCO to let me know what to do'.

'Wait, do we have a SENDCO?'

Look, if you have used any variations of the above phrases or heard a colleague or two use these phrases then we need to reset the relational link between them and the SENDCO.

Why?

The rather ominous phrase 'we are all teachers of SEND' is so vividly true, yet so obscure too. Essentially it places the responsibility of teaching students with additional needs at the heart of every educator. The very principle of inclusion is that students should be educated alongside their peers where possible and through a whole school commitment to meeting the needs of diverse students. Yet, despite this universally recognised principle, there is a specific and distinct role in every school that is set up primarily to ensure that the effective inclusion of these students is occurring.

So, how do you effectively work with your SENDCO and other key individuals to apply the core principles of inclusion? Well, The SEND Code of Practice (GOV.UK, 2014) describes the role of the Special Educational Needs Coordinator in schools as someone whose responsibility includes coordinating provision for students with SEND and providing support to colleagues. This reflects the idea that supporting students with SEND is a collective effort.

As I present the following information, I want you to **reflect** on how you can involve yourself in those areas and how it will benefit your students. Using this table as an example, create something similar where you can write down how you might positively contribute to the work SENCO does. I've started you off with some examples.

Parts of the SENDCO role	What this means for the SENDCO	How I can contribute – example
Coordination	SENDCOs are responsible for coordinating the provision and support for students with SEND, ensuring that their needs are met effectively	Collaborate with the SENDCO to ensure effective coordination of support for students with SEND by following pupil passports/pupil profile/learning plans (or whatever your SENDCO calls them!)
		If you can suggest additions/ amendments, do so
Assessment	Oversee the assessment and identification of students with SEND, working with teachers to gather relevant information and provide guidance on the assessment process	Provide relevant information when required and collaborate with the SENDCO during the assessment and identification process for students with SEND
Support and training	SENDCOs provide guidance and support to teachers in implementing strategies and interventions for students with SEND. They may also offer training and resources to help teachers better meet the needs of these students	Participate in training sessions offered by the SENDCO and implement strategies and interventions as recommended. Provide feedback as to how they are working

(Continued)

(Continued)

Parts of the SENDCO role	What this means for the SENDCO	How I can contribute – example
Individualised plans	SENDCOs work with teachers to develop and review individualised education plans (IEPs) or Pupil Profiles/Passports/ Learning Plans for students with SEND, ensuring that teaching strategies are tailored to each student's unique needs	Work closely with the SENDCO to develop and regularly review individualised education plans (IEPs) or Section F elements of an EHCP
Liaison	They serve as a crucial link between teachers, parents, external agencies, and professionals, facilitating communication and collaboration to provide the best possible support for students with SEND	Know which agencies are involved with your students and use their advice and guidance where relevant. Attend a meeting too?

Remember they're SENDCOs not MENDCOs – they can't fix everything themselves. That was really bad wasn't it? MENDCO... I am sorry!

A SENDCO's role is complex, deep ranging and all consuming – go and say thank you to your SENDCO today, it really can be a very lonely role. And if you're feeling missed out, here is a thank you from me, especially for reading this book to help you fulfil your inclusive duties for your students. (Whilst you're saying thank you, go and thank your Designated Safeguarding Lead too – DSL. It is usually the same person!)

TEACHING ASSISTANTS/LEARNING SUPPORT ASSISTANTS

Well, if you are lucky enough to have a Teaching Assistant (TA) or a Learning Support Assistant (the absolute heroes in education), then we need to establish ways of working that are both mutually beneficial but also impactful for your young people.

Here are my top five tips:

1. Know and remember their name and refer to them as an equal in the classroom – they are teaching assistants, not your assistant. Subtle difference. Maybe this is aimed more at secondary school colleagues, who may have different TAs in different lessons, as opposed to Primary and Special schools, along with Pupil Referral Units, that will have more fixed teams of TAs in regular lessons.

2. Allocate roles and ensure there is clarity. Contract in advance the specifics of your classroom.

3. Provide information for pre-teaching, overlearning and support, in advance. Do this in an understandable format, don't **just** give Schemes of Work as these are written by teachers, for teachers.

4. Provide time for the information you have provided to be used effectively.

5. Ask for feedback. Ask your TA regularly whether the instructions you gave were clear, accessible, or even whether the visual items you used were understandable, for example.

The Education Endowment Foundation has produced numerous resources on working with TAs (for example, Education Endowment Foundation, 2021). They provide useful summaries and recommendations on working with TAs. I would strongly recommend downloading the Recommendations Poster and sticking it on your wall, and working out what you will Try, Refine and Ditch from these seven powerful suggestions.

PARENTS AND CARERS

If you have been in education for a few years or so, then I am sure you will have heard the phrase 'hard to reach'. I am not comfortable with this, as it is without doubt that many, often from my own personal community, will potentially be hit with this label. Are families really hard to reach or are we as schools not willing to listen? Or maybe schools are hard to approach?

Do not forget parents and carers know your students better than you. Call them, meet them, ask for their advice, and learn top do's and don'ts too! Don't wait until things are going very wrong, or something negative has occurred; be proactive.

Ofsted's most recent research and analysis report on Support SEND was updated in May 2021. Rather surprisingly the SEND analysis mentions parents 175 times, which is encouraging to see as their involvement is an integral approach to effective SEND provision.

> Collaboration between practitioners and families supported schools in meeting pupils' needs more effectively.

Is it that simple? Just work together to help students experiencing difficulties? Essentially, yes. Well then there is no need to read on, right? Well, not quite. Just talking about what the school can and can't offer is not communication. That is a one-way conversation. The ideal is **co-production**. This is when parents are involved in a child's support, their plan, their targets, their provision. This can be done as part of a student's reviews across the year or in response to certain situations that crop up. Why have we not fixed this problem yet? Yes, of course, some parents do not engage with schools, but that is a small minority. So why is it that the 2019 House of Commons Education Select Committee report has highlighted that 'parents, children and young people were often not meaningfully involved in decision-making and reviews' (GOV.UK, 2021)?

So, I have highlighted the problem, what can you and I do about it? Well, here are some strategies that can be short, medium and long term, and can be both high impact and high effort, depending on your context and the stage of your journey.

⬚ HINTS AND TIPS

- Create a parent forum – organise a termly meeting for parents to come and discuss provision. Think carefully about the time of these forums; think about the location, how accessible are they? Don't make them formal, consider the language you use to invite and bring parents on board.

- Simplify the coordination of internal and external services/ provisions by creating a Frequently Asked Question document(s), make video explanations, virtual tours, provide visual representations of key information. It's important to remember that parents and carers want transparency and accountability in SEND provision. The IPSEA website explains numerous legal requirements imposed on schools and for parents (IPSEA, n.d.).

- Remember and remind yourself that transition is not just from Primary to Secondary school, it is also between each year group or moving between class levels; meet, discuss, explain, and show how the curriculum is changing and how aspirations remain high whilst adaptations are ongoing.

SPECIAL SCHOOLS

In England, special schools play a crucial role in providing education and support to students with SEND. These schools are designed to meet the unique needs of students who may require more specialised teaching approaches and resources. The support provided by special schools in England can vary based on the individual needs of the students, but here are some common ways in which these schools offer assistance:

Individualised Education Plans (IEPs) (or Personalised Learning Plans or whatever iteration of this term schools are using): Special schools typically develop individualised plans for each student, outlining their specific learning needs, goals and strategies for support. These are regularly reviewed and updated to ensure they address the evolving needs of the student.

Specialised teaching staff: Special schools often have teachers and staff with expertise in working with students with a range of special educational needs. This includes professionals trained in areas such as autism spectrum conditions, dyslexia, ADHD, and other learning or physical disabilities.

Smaller class sizes: Special schools tend to have smaller class sizes to provide more individualised attention to students. This allows teachers to tailor their teaching methods to suit the learning styles and pace of each student.

Specialised curriculum: The curriculum in special schools is adapted to meet the diverse needs of students. It may include a combination of academic subjects, life skills and therapies designed to support the development of each student.

Therapeutic support: Special schools often have access to therapeutic services, including speech and language therapy, occupational therapy and counselling. These services are integrated into the students' overall educational plan.

Adapted learning resources: Special schools provide learning resources that are adapted to meet the needs of students with various disabilities. This may include materials in alternative formats, assistive technology and sensory equipment.

Emphasis on social and emotional development: Special schools recognise the importance of social and emotional development. They often incorporate programs and activities that focus on building social skills, fostering self-esteem, and promoting positive behaviour.

Parental/carer involvement: Special schools encourage active involvement from parents/carers. Regular communication, parent/carer–teacher meetings and collaboration in the development and review of IEPs help ensure a holistic approach to the student's education.

Transition planning: Special schools may assist students in transition planning, preparing them for the next stage of their education or for life after school. This could include vocational training, employment support, or further education.

It's important to note that the support provided can vary between different special schools, and each school tailors its approach to meet the specific needs of its student population. The goal is to create a nurturing and inclusive learning environment that enables every student to reach their full potential. Special schools and indeed Pupil Referral Units are the unsung heroes of our education system, in many cases underfunded, stretched and forgotten about in Education discourse.

 # REFLECTION

Have you visited your local special school or Pupil Referral Unit? Do you know if there is one? Find out and arrange a visit. Go and observe, non-judgmentally, but developmentally. See what you can pick up.

Could you arrange an interchange of CPD where they come to your school for CPD, and you go over there for CPD too? This might be something you want to suggest to your SLT.

NOTE IT DOWN

THINK ABOUT THE NEXT PARENT/CARER MEETING YOU ARE
GOING TO HAVE. USING THE SPACE BELOW, JOT DOWN WAYS
IN WHICH YOU CAN BE MORE EFFICIENT AND EFFECTIVE
HAVING PAID ATTENTION TO THE INFORMATION IN THIS
CHAPTER.

CHAPTER 6
SOME HELPFUL RESOURCES

So, there we have it, a *Little Guide for Teachers: SEND in School*. Throughout this book I have just tried to share with you some strategies, ideas and thoughts that are hopefully low effort and high impact.

I have spent many years thinking that teachers need to differentiate, adapt and just do better, but that's simply not true. We as educators need to ensure we know **how** to differentiate, **what** to differentiate and **for whom** to differentiate. There is a subtle difference between differentiating and scaffolding. Scaffolding requires support to eventually be suspended, removed, thus allowing for self-fulfilment from the child/student/young person. Differentiation may be needed throughout a child's education journey, and that is OK. What is not OK is lowering your expectations of what is achievable and comprehensible.

Don't just expect expectations but model, repeat and remind them of these ideals, these processes and strategies.

It is worth noting that the Pygmalion Effect or the Rosenthal and Jacobson Effect (Rosenthal and Jacobson, 1968) describes that positive expectations influence performance. Equally if you have negative viewpoints about your students, even subconsciously it will have an adverse effect. This is known as the Golem Effect or the Reverse Pygmalion Effect (Babad, Inbar, and Rosenthal, 1982). Or in simpler terms, a self-fulfilling prophecy as they work both ways!

I have flooded you with ideas. I have asked you to consider what you will Try, Refine and Ditch (based on what you are currently doing). I have helped structure your implementation intentions by asking you to identify which of your thoughts are short, medium or long term. By doing this, you can think, plan and turn steps into actions, actions into goals! And finally, expertise. I will never claim to be an expert, but I have a small amount of expertise in this area and I have an overwhelming desire, passion and drive for others to have more expertise. I am therefore hoping you can use these ideas in this book to create your own CPD programmes, T&L breakfasts, bulletins and newsletters, and that you can share these ideas with others.

Thank you for reading and thank you sincerely for your time.

To further support you on your journey, I have listed organisations and resources below.

Organisation name	Description/role
ADHD Foundation	Support, resources and advocacy for individuals with ADHD
APD Support UK	Provides free information about Auditory Processing Disorder (APD) and links to support for living with this condition
Autism Education Trust	Aiming to ensure that autistic children and young people receive education that helps them fulfil their aspirations and engage in society as active citizens
British Dyslexia Association	Resources and support for dyslexic individuals
Cerebral Palsy Foundation	Support for individuals with cerebral palsy and their families
Children in Wales SEND	Advocates for children's rights and provides support for children with SEN and their families in Wales
Council for Disabled Children	Serves as the umbrella body for the disabled children's sector, bringing together professionals, practitioners and policymakers
Department for Education (DfE)	Sets policies and guidelines for SEN in education
Disabled Living	Offers impartial information about services for disabled individuals, older people and their supporters, including advice about products and equipment
Down's Syndrome Association	Information and support for individuals with Down's syndrome
Dyspraxia Foundation	Support for individuals with dyspraxia
Epilepsy Action	Information and support for individuals with epilepsy
Heads Together	A mental health initiative working to change the conversation on mental health and provide innovative services

(Continued)

(Continued)

Organisation name	Description/role
Inclusion Ireland	Advocates for the rights and inclusion of people with intellectual disabilities in Irish society
Independent Provider of Special Education Advice (IPSEA)	Offers free legal advice and support for parents and carers on SEN issues
Irish Deaf Society	Advocates for the rights of deaf people in Ireland
Irish Learning Support Association	Supports professionals working with students with additional educational needs in Ireland
Irish Society for Autism	Support and information for autistic individuals and their families in Ireland
Look UK	A small national charity providing support and information for visually impaired young people, their carers and families
Mind	Provides advice and support to empower individuals experiencing mental health problems
NAS (National Autistic Society)	The UK's leading charity for people on the autism spectrum and their families
Nasen (National Association for Special Educational Needs)	A charitable membership organisation supporting those working with children and young people with SEND and learning differences
National Deaf Children's Society (NDCS)	The leading charity for deaf children in the UK
NHS Children's Speech and Language Therapy Resources	Provides resources for children's speech and language therapy

Organisation name	Description/role
NSPCC (National Society for the Prevention of Cruelty to Children)	The UK's leading children's charity, focused on child protection and well-being
RADLD (Raising Awareness of Developmental Language Disorder)	Focuses on raising awareness of Developmental Language Disorder
RNIB (Royal National Institute of Blind People)	A leading sight loss charity providing support for blind and partially sighted individuals
RNIB Bookshare	Provides accessible textbooks and resources for learners with various disabilities, including sight loss, dyslexia, dyspraxia and autism
SEN Together	Support, advice and resources for parents and carers of children with SEN in Northern Ireland
SENDIAS (Special Educational Needs and Disabilities Information, Advice and Support Services)	Provides information, advice and support to parents and carers of children with SEN
SEND Unlocked Directory	Offers information, advice and guidance on accessing support and services available to the SEND community
Sibs	The UK charity for people who grow up with a disabled brother or sister
Sight Advice	A collaborative resource from multiple organisations, offering advice and information for children, young people and families affected by sight loss
SOSEN	Offers a free, confidential telephone helpline for parents and others seeking information and advice on Special Educational Needs and Disability (SEND)

(Continued)

(Continued)

Organisation name	Description/role
Special Needs Jungle	A resource aiming to empower families by providing information, tips and resources to navigate the complex system of special educational needs
Young Epilepsy	Supports children and young people with epilepsy
YoungMinds	A charity dedicated to improving the mental health of children and young people in the UK

Here are some useful podcasts too – I am just trying to be young, cool, and down with the new trends!

Podcast name	Description/topics
InspirEDucate	Discusses various aspects of education, including SEN
SEN Jigsaw	Issues related to SEN in mainstream schools
SENDcast	Various aspects of SEN, interviews with experts
SENDcast – What Matters to Me	Personal stories from parents, carers and individuals with SEN
SPELD NZ Dyslexia Talk Podcast	Insights into supporting dyslexic students
Teaching With SEND in Mind	Strategies for creating inclusive classrooms
Tales from the Teacher's Chair	Stories and insights from teachers, including those working with SEN

You can explore these podcasts on your preferred podcast platform for episodes that align with your interests and professional development needs in SEND teaching.

Keep note of this table below which contains **some** of the many acronyms you might see, read or hear in relation to students with special educational needs. This list has been provided to demonstrate how varied supporting our students is. There will no doubt be some changes and adaptations as language develops. Remember this is not an exhaustive list but a sample of the varying complexities in SEND!

Acronym	Description
ACE	Adverse Childhood Experiences are potentially traumatic or stressful childhood experiences
ADHD/ADD	Attention Deficit Hyperactivity Disorder is a neurological condition that affects concentration and ability to focus
AEN	Additional Educational Needs, an alternative phrase to group any additional difficulties that one may face in their learning – used commonly in Wales
ALNCO	Additional Learning Needs Coordinator – used in Wales and Ireland for example
AP	Alternative Provision supplied instead of mainstream school
ASC/D	Autism Spectrum Condition/Autism Spectrum Disorder, a neurological, developmental condition that affects the way one sees, behaves, learns and interacts with others
ASN	Additional Support Needs, an alternative phrase to group any additional difficulties that one may face in their learning – used commonly in Scotland
BESD	Behavioural, Emotional, Social Difficulties; this acronym was effectively replaced by SEMH in the new SEND code of practice
BSL	British Sign Language, the most common form of sign language
CAMHS	Child and Adolescent Mental Health Services supporting people including mental health difficulties
CATs	Cognitive Ability Tests are used to ascertain a student's reasoning and thinking skills
C&I	Communication and Interaction is a term used to encompass people with speech, language and communication needs

(Continued)

(Continued)

Acronym	Description
CoP (SEND)	Code of Practice, the current legal frameworks underpinning SEND provision
DfE	Department For Education, the organisation responsible for educational provision in the UK
DLA	Disability Living Allowance is a social security benefit granted to parents/carers who have children with disabilities
EAL	English as an Additional Language, a descriptor used to label students who do not have English as their first language
EHCP	Education, Health and Care Plan, the legal entitlement for a young person listing out their provision in education, health and care grounds
EP	Educational Psychologists use their knowledge in psychology and child development to support students and schools
GLD	Global Learning Delay is where a child might take longer to reach developmental milestones
HLTA	Higher Level Teaching Assistant, a qualification-based label/job
IEP	Individual Education Plan, a plan that sets out targets and strategies to help children learn
KS	Key Stages are differing stages or blocks of the national curriculum
LAC/CLA	Looked After Child/Child Looked After, a child not living with their biological parents
LO	Local Offers provide information and support to young people in their locality
MLD	Moderate Learning Difficulty affecting a student's learning, moderately
MSI	Multi-Sensory Impairment, including a loss of two or more senses, such as deafblind could be known as dual sensory impaired

Acronym	Description
OT	Occupational Therapists support people with injuries, illnesses or disabilities
PDA/ODD	Pathological Demand Avoidance/Oppositional Demand Disorder is a characteristic where avoidance of demands and requirements are regular and argued to be unavoidable
PEEP	Personal Emergency Evacuation Plan, used to provide details in case of an evacuation being needed in the event of a fire or lockdown
PEP	Personal Educational Plan used for Looked after Children (LAC) – many prefer CIC (Child/ren in Care).
PMLD	Profound multiple learning difficulties could include people having severe difficulties with seeing, hearing or moving
PP/PPG	Pupil Premium Grant, an additional amount of money provided to support students whose parents/carers are below an economic threshold
PRU	Pupil Referral Units are a type of school that caters for children who aren't able to attend a mainstream school
SALT/SLT	Speech and Language Therapist (NOT Senior Leadership Team!), trained individuals who help people with communication, eating, swallowing and drinking
SEMH	Social, Emotional, Mental Health, a state of difficulty in managing behaviours and emotions
SENDIASS	Special Educational Needs and Disability Information Advice and Support Service used to help parents/carers
SENDIST	Special Educational Needs and Disability Tribunal services for parents/carers
SENCO/ SENDCO/ ALNCO	Special Educational Needs Coordinator/Special Educational Needs and Disabilities Coordinator/Additional Learning Needs Coordinator
SLD	Severe Learning Difficulty, similar to PMLD, but usually diagnosed at birth

(Continued)

(Continued)

Acronym	Description
SpLD	Specific Learning Difficulty include ASD/ASC, dyslexia, dysgraphia and other neurological conditions
TA/LSA	Teaching Assistant/Learning Support Assistant, adults used to provide support in and out of classrooms Remember the subtle difference between a teaching assistant and a teacher's assistant!
VI	Visual Impairments including colour blindness, blurred vision and Irlen's syndrome

The next table provides an overview of the key elements of PDA and practical strategies for teachers to support students with these challenges in the classroom.

Key elements	Description	What you can do about it
1. Excessive anxiety and avoidance	Students experience extreme anxiety when faced with demands and respond with avoidance behaviours like procrastination or refusal	Provide a structured, predictable environment Offer clear and concise instructions Use visuals to support understanding Allow for a form of break to reduce anxiety
2. Resistance to everyday demands	Students may resist routine or seemingly simple tasks, such as following instructions, completing tasks, or participating in classroom routines	Present tasks in a non-confrontational manner Offer choices and flexibility in how tasks are completed Use positive reinforcement and rewards for cooperation

Key elements	Description	What you can do about it
3. Need for control	PDA individuals need a sense of control. Teachers can support by offering choices and maintaining structure while allowing flexibility	Incorporate elements of choices within the classroom routine Establish clear boundaries and expectations Provide advance notice of changes or transitions
4. Social communication challenges	Students with PDA may struggle with social communication. Teachers should create low-demand opportunities for communication and provide visual support	Use non-verbal communication cues (e.g., visual schedules) Encourage one-on-one or small-group interactions Be patient and allow time for responses
5. Fluctuating presentation	Behaviours and capabilities can vary from day to day. Teachers should be patient, adaptable, and tailor their approach to the student's current state	Be flexible in expectations and approaches Monitor and adapt to the student's daily or moment-to-moment needs Collaborate with specialists or support staff as needed

Now your turn… use the prompt to search for more information. When you find something, you then need to write down what you will Try, Refine or Ditch for your lessons next week based on the further information you found! Better still, what information will you share with others? In my experience the best way to do this is to share and show how the idea will benefit that teacher and their lessons.

BIBLIOGRAPHY

Babad, E.Y., Inbar, J., and Rosenthal, R. (1982). 'Pygmalion, Galatea, and the Golem: Investigations of biased and unbiased teachers'. *Journal of Educational Psychology*, 74 (4): 459.

Billington, G. and Meadows, M. (2005). *A review of literature on marking reliability*. Available at: https://filestore.aqa.org.uk/content/research/CERP_RP_MM_01052005.pdf (accessed 7 March 2024).

Brighouse, T. (2006). *Essential pieces: A jigsaw of a successful school*. Didcot: Research Machines.

Brighouse, T. and Woods, D. (2013). *A–Z of school improvement*. London: Bloomsbury Publishing.

British Dyslexia Association (n.d.). *Dyslexia friendly style guide*. Available at: www.bdadyslexia.org.uk/advice/employers/creating-a-dyslexia-friendly-work place/dyslexia-friendly-style-guide (accessed 7 March 2024).

Citizen School (2020). *6 step guide to change*. Available at: https://citizen-school.files.wordpress.com/2020/09/blm-protocols-citizen-school.pdf (accessed 7 March 2024).

Cowley, S. (2018). *The ultimate guide to differentiation*. London: Bloomsbury Publishing.

Dix, P. (2017). *When the adults change everything changes*. Carmarthen: Crown House Publishing.

Education Endowment Foundation (2021). *Making best use of teaching assistants*. Available at: https://educationendowmentfoundation.org.uk/education-evidence/guidance-reports/teaching-assistants (accessed 7 March 2024).

Evidence-Based Teaching (2023). *The I do we do you do model explained*. Available at: www.evidencebasedteaching.org.au/the-i-do-we-do-you-do-model-explained/ (accessed 7 March 2024).

GOV.UK (n.d.). *Equality Act 2010*. Available at: www.legislation.gov.uk/ukp-ga/2010/15/contents (accessed 7 March 2024).

GOV.UK (2014). *SEND code of practice: 0 to 25 years*. Available at: www.gov.uk/government/publications/send-code-of-practice-0-to-25 (accessed 7 March 2024).

GOV.UK (2021). *Supporting SEND*. Available at: www.gov.uk/government/publications/supporting-send/supporting-send (accessed 20 May 2024).

GOV.UK (2023a). *Schools, pupils and their characteristics, academic year 2022/23*. Available at: https://explore-education-statistics.service.gov.uk/find-statistics/school-pupils-and-their-characteristics (accessed 7 March 2024).

GOV.UK (2023b). *Special educational needs in England, academic year 2022/23*. Available at: https://explore-education-statistics.service.gov.uk/find-statistics/special-educational-needs-in-england (accessed 7 March 2024).

Carol Gray – Social Stories (2024). Available at: https://carolgraysocialstories.com (accessed 20 May 2024).

IPSEA (Independent Provider of Special Education Advice) (n.d.). *SEN and disability statute law, regulations and guidance*. Available at: www.ipsea.

org.uk/sen-and-disability-statute-law-regulations-and-guidance (accessed 7 March 2024).

Jaime, O.T. (n.d.). *Positioning in the classroom*. Available at: https://missjaimeot.com/positioning-in-the-classroom/ (accessed 7 March 2024).

JCQ (Joint Council for Qualifications) (n.d.). *Access arrangements, reasonable adjustments and special consideration*. Available at: www.jcq.org.uk/exams-office/access-arrangements-and-special-consideration/ (accessed 7 March 2024).

Lindsay, G., Pather, S. and Strand, S. (2006). *Special educational needs and ethnicity: Issues of over- and under-representation*. Available at: www.naldic.org.uk/Resources/NALDIC/Research%20and%20Information/Documents/RR757.pdf (accessed 7 March 2024).

Milestones Autism Resources (2024). *The 5-point scale: A tool to learn emotions and calming strategies*. Available at: https://www.milestones.org/map/browse-articles/the-5-point-scale-a-tool-to-learn-emotions-and-calming-strategies (accessed 7 March 2024).

NALDIC (2015). *EAL resource library*. Available at: https://www.naldic.org.uk/eal-teaching-and-learning/eal-resources/ (accessed 7 March 2024).

National Autistic Society (2024). *Different behaviour between school and home*. Available at: www.autism.org.uk/advice-and-guidance/topics/education/different-behaviour-between-school-and-home/parents-and-carers (accessed 7 March 2024).

Rosenthal, R. and Jacobson, L. (1968). 'Pygmalion in the classroom'. *The Urban Review* 3, 16–20. https://doi.org/10.1007/BF02322211

Shire (2018). *Teaching and managing students with ADHD: Systems, strategies, solutions.* Available at: https://www.adhdfoundation.org.uk/wp-content/uploads/2022/03/Teaching-and-Managing-Students-with-ADHD.pdf (accessed 20 May 2024).

Special Needs Jungle (2022). *Intersectionality in SEND: Families experiences in schools.* Available at: www.specialneedsjungle.com/wp-content/uploads/2022/03/Race-and-SEND-Survey_Final_170322.pdf (accessed 7 March 2024).

Strand, S. and Lindorff, A. (2018). *Ethnic disproportionality in the identification of Special Educational Needs (SEN) in England: Extent, causes and consequences.* Oxford: Oxford University Press.

The Swann Report (1985): Education for All (1985). Available at https://www.education uk.org/documents/swann/swann1985.html (accessed 20 May 2024).

Vygotsky, L. S. (1978). *Mind in Society: the Development of Higher Psychological Processes.* Cambridge, MA: Harvard University Press.

INDEX

acronyms, 73–6
ADHD, 52–5
assessment, 59
assumptions, 36, 37
audio content, 20
auditory processing, 51
autism, 47–50

Behavioural, Emotional and
    Social difficulties (BESD/
    SEMHD), 8, 33
biases, 36
British Dyslexia Association, 15, 51

carers *see* parents and carers
chunking, 16
class sizes, 64
classroom environment, 21–2, 47,
    53, 54
closed captions, 20
co-production, 62
codes, 6, 8
Cognition and Learning (C&L)
    needs, 7
cognitive flexibility, 26
comic strip conversations, 48
communication, and ADHD, 53–4
Communication and Interaction
    (C&I) needs, 7
comprehending, 19–21
concentration, 51
coordination of provision, 59
curriculum, 64

de-escalation plans, 49
decoding, 15–19
differentiation, 68
discussion, 20
dyslexia, 15, 50–2

E code, 6, 8
EAL (English as an Additional
    Language), 9, 33
Education Endowment
    Foundation, 61
Educational Health Care Plan
    (EHCP), 8–9
effort, 13
emotional development, 64
emotional regulation, 26
emotions, recognising, 47–8
English as an Additional Language
    (EAL), 9, 33
environment
    and neurodiversity, 47, 53, 54
    for writing, 21–2
*Ethnic Disproportionality
    in the Identification of Special
    Educational Needs (SEN)
    in England* (Strand &
    Lindorff), 32–3
ethnic minority groups
    parent/carer voice, 36–7
    representation, 32–6
    strategies, 38–41
executive functioning skills, 25–7
expectations, 12, 68

feedback, 46, 54, 61
focus, 51

gender, 33
goal setting, 27
Golem Effect, 68
Gypsy/Roma pupils, 34
    see also Traveller communities

handwriting, 24
hearing impairment, 33
highlighting, 17

'I do, we do, you do' model, 23
inclusion, 58
individualised education plans
        (IEPs), 60, 63–4
information, for parents and
        carers, 63
intersectionality, 32, 34
Intersectionality in SEND (Special
        Needs Jungle), 34

K code, 6, 8

learning barriers, 14–15
    listening and comprehending,
        19–21
    reading and decoding, 15–19
    time management, 24–8
    writing, 21–4
learning difficulties, 7
learning resources, in special
        schools, 64
learning support assistants, 61
legislation, 6
liaison, 60
Lindorff, A., 32–3
Lindsay, G., 33–4
listening and comprehending,
        19–21

marginalised groups
    parent/carer voice, 36–7
    representation, 32–6
    strategies, 38–41
maximum output, 13
memory, 26, 50
modelling, 23

narration of learning, 23
need categories, 6–8, 9
neurodiversity, 46
    ADHD, 52–5
    autism, 47–50
    dyslexia, 15, 50–2
non-examples, 22

organisation and planning,
        26, 60, 65
    see also routines and processes
organisations, 69–72
output, 13

parent forums, 63
parents and carers
    involved in special schools, 64
    relationships with, 62–3
    voice, 36–7
pathological demand avoidance
        (PDA), 76–7
Physical and/or Sensory Needs
        (P&SN), 8
physical resources, 47
planning and organisation,
        26, 50, 65
    see also routines and processes
podcasts, 72
pre-teaching, 16, 19–20, 61
processing time, 25
pupil profiles/passports/learning
        plans, 60
Pygmalion Effect, 68

readability, 15, 18
reading, 15–19, 51
reading ages/levels, 16–17, 18
reasonable adjustments, 6
recordings, transcribed, 20
reflection, 41
relationships
  with parents and carers, 62–3
  with SENDCOs, 58–60
  with teaching assistants, 61
repeating information, 20–1
representation issues, 32–6
  strategies, 38–41
resources
  acronyms, 73–6
  physical, 47
  podcasts, 72
  for reading and decoding,
    17–18
  in special schools, 64
  support organisations, 69–72
Reverse Pygmalion Effect, 68
Rosenthal and Jacobsen Effect, 68
routines and processes, 47, 54
ruler line guides, 16

scaffolding, 68
self-control, 26
self-fulfilling prophecy, 68
self-monitoring, 27
SEND *see* Special Educational Needs
    and Disabilities
SEND Code of Practice (SEND CoP), 6
SENDCOs, 58–60
sequencing, 16, 21
social development, 64
Social, Emotional and Mental Health
    difficulties (SEMHD/BESD),
    8, 33
social stories, 48
socio-economic disadvantage, 33

Special Educational Needs
    Coordinators (SENDCOs),
    58–60
Special Educational Needs and
    Disabilities (SEND)
  acronyms, 73–6
  categories of need, 6–8, 9
  legislation, 6
  podcasts, 72
  shifting approaches to, 1–2
  support organisations, 69–72
*Special Educational Needs and
    Ethnicity* (Lindsay), 33–4
Special Needs Jungle, 32, 34
special schools, 63–5
specific learning difficulties
    (SpLDs), 7
  see also ADHD; autism; dyslexia
Speech, Communication and
    Language Needs (SCLN), 7
stereotypes, 37
Strand, S., 32–3
stress scales, 47–8, 49
subtitles, 20
success, 12
support
  from SENDCOS, 59
  organisations, 69–72
  podcasts, 72
  see also resources
Swan Report (1985), 34

task initiation, 26
teaching assistants, 61
teaching staff, in special
    schools, 64
terminology, 73–6
therapeutic support, in special
    schools, 64
'Think, Pair, Share' strategy, 20
thinking time, 25

time management, 24–8, 51
timers, 25
tools
   for reading and decoding,
      17–18
   see also resources
training, 59
transcripts of audio content, 20
transition planning, 65
Traveller communities,
   34, 39–41
'try, refine, ditch' approach, 4–5,
   18–19, 21, 24, 28, 52

underlining, 17

video subtitles, 20
visual aids, 16
visual processing, 50
vocabulary, pre-teaching,
   16, 19–20

working memory, 26
writing, 21–4, 50
writing position, 22

Zone of Proximal Development, 13